# G.O.

Get Unstuck & Move Toward Your Dreams

## TYMETRIC DILLON

Scripture verses depicting KJV and AMP are taken from The King James and Amplified Parallel Bible, © 2011 by Zondervan Publishing Company, Grand Rapids, Michigan 49546, USA. All rights reserved.

G.O.
Get Unstuck & Move Toward Your Dreams

Copyright © 2017 By Tymetric Dillon
ISBN 978-1-946683-95-3
Library of Congress Control Number 2017939196

Published by Rapier Publishing Company
260 W. Main Street, Suite #1
Dothan, Alabama 36301
www.rapierpublishing.com

All rights reserved under the International Copyright Law. No part of this publication may be reproduced, stored in a retrieval system, or transmitted in any form or by any means electronic, mechanical, photocopy, or any other means without the prior permission of the publisher or author except for brief quotations embodied in reviews and articles as they relate to the book.

First Edition
Printed in the United States of America.

Contact Tymetric Dillon @: www.tymetricdillon.com
Tymetric Dillon Enterprises
P.O. Box 1305 Gadsden, Alabama 35902

Book Cover Design: Adrian Simpson @ www.dominiongraphicdesign.com
Book Interior Layout: Rapture Graphics.
Book Exterior Layout: Garrett Myers.

*The views expressed in this work are solely those of the author and do not necessarily reflect the views of the publisher, and the publisher hereby disclaims any responsibility for them.*

*This book is dedicated to my beautiful wife Tanisha & my children Trinity, Taniyah and Ty Jr. Every day of my life is amazing because God gave me you. When I look into your eyes it reminds me that I can GO take on the world. I love you more than words can say!*

# ACKNOWLEDGMENTS

Thank you to:
Myrtle Dillon (Mom) and Fannie, for challenging me to do great things;
Apostle Amos and Yolanda Howard and the Howard family for guidance, love and support;
Living Truth Christian Center, for allowing me to serve you;
Lawrence and Jewel Presley, for your example of perseverance;
Cheryl Griffith, for editing the early manuscript;
Adrian Simpson, for great graphic design and website;
Michelle Funderburg and Tanisha Dillon, for transcribing the first draft; and
Pete and Fannie Pierce and Rapier Publishing for partnering with me to bring this book to life.

# CONTENTS

Foreword
Preface ............................................................. 11
Introduction .................................................... 15
   1. GOD ONLY ............................................ 17
   2. GRAND OUTLOOK ......................... 20
   3. GAGE OPPOSITION ........................ 24
   4. GET OFFENSIVE ............................... 27
   5. GIFTS OPERATING ......................... 31
   6. GET OUT ........................................... 35
   7. GLEAN & OBSERVE ........................ 40
   8. GOODBYE OBVIOUS ..................... 43
   9. GOALS & OBJECTIVES ................... 47
  10. GRAMMATICAL ONENESS ............ 50
  11. GUIDED OPTICS ............................. 53
  12. GUARD OPENINGS ........................ 57
  13. GRADE OPINIONS .......................... 61
  14. GENUINE & OFFICIAL ................... 65
  15. GATHER OTHERS ........................... 70
  16. GAG OFFENSE ................................. 75
  17. GROW OLDER ................................. 79
  18. GRAB ON .......................................... 83
  19. GOD OPPORTUNITIES .................. 87
  20. GRIND OBSESSIVELY ..................... 92
Conclusion ..................................................... 97

# FOREWORD

GO, Get Unstuck and Move Toward Your Dreams, will challenge, charge and change your life. Having said that, I do have to confess that it's very hard for me to write an unbiased forward for my son, Tymetric Dillon's first of many books. First I must say, I am a proud Father who has watched Ty get unstuck and walk out his God-given purpose in so many areas of his life. Life has its problems, pressures and pains that can cause speed bumps or stop signs that will slow us down, sideline us or even get us stuck. How we handle these moments become a defining moment in our lives. We can choose to be depressed, distracted, disappointed or discouraged and take a detour or we can deploy the strategies in this book and once again get moving toward destiny. Ty really challenges us to look at the bigger picture. I believe what he says, "the grand outlook which helps one push past the problem, pain and pressures to see the end of a thing." The Bible is clear in Ecclesiastes 7:8 NIV, "…the end of a matter is better than its beginning, and the patience is better than pride." In Job 8:7 KJV, "Though thy beginning was small, yet thy latter end should greatly increase." Simply put, take the challenge to get unstuck, and go for it. I don't know what your "it" is, but in the words of Ty, Dream Big. After reading this book, it not only challenged me to search areas where I had become complacent, but it charged me to pick up the broken pieces and get moving again. This book, I believe, will be a breath of fresh air that will refresh, revive, renew and restore your faith to know that life is full of pitfalls but your purpose is bigger and stronger than anything the enemy might do to try to impede your progress. I thank God for this mighty Man of God obeying the Holy Spirit and writing this life-changing book. If you follow the simple but profound wisdom found in this book, you too will become wealthy beyond your wildest imagination. Remember, God will give you more on your way than when you start. Now Go and Enjoy!

Apostle Amos L. Howard, Sr.

## PREFACE

Thursday, July 7, 2016 marked a very tragic day in current American history. After several young men had been killed by law enforcement earlier in the week, five Dallas, TX police officers were shot and killed in an ambush. The country was in an uproar at what appeared to be retaliation for the recent shootings of unarmed black men by police. It seemed as if we were in an all-out war!

How would we move past this? Protest broke out all across the country. Major corridors where people traveled in and out of cities were blocked by human barricades. People had had enough, and this was their way of showing it. But, how effective would it be? What were the objectives? What would change as a result of the time, energy, and resources that are spent? I began to notice that after the marching things went back to business as usual. People had jobs, businesses and families that they had to attend to. Even if their hearts wanted to continue, their lives were not conducive to them being absent for an extended period of time without feeling the effects. I began to think; if something as horrific as this didn't cause people to galvanize and go, what would? I didn't understand it. We can protest and get no progress. We can march yet never move.

A few months later my daughter started kindergarten. It was very emotional because it seemed like yesterday that her mother and I had brought her home from the hospital. Then a few weeks later she turned five years old. Ten days later my second daughter turned two years old. Next, I had a birthday, and I realized how close I was getting to being 40 years old. Then I began to think about my son, who had not been born yet, but was due within a few months. All of these things caused me to take a very thorough inventory of my life and how far I had moved from my starting point. Then it hit me like a ton of bricks! I was doing the same thing as those that I criticized months earlier. If someone were to look at me, they would see that I was busy doing a number of things. I was making progress, but there were areas in my life that I was marking time in one spot rather than moving forward to the rhythm of life. At that moment I settled that I wasn't willing to live life with regrets and that it was time for my family and me to GO after all God has planned for us.

No group of people, including families, will ever progress without there first being personal progression in the individual. Progress must be made from the inside out. Even in the case of police brutality and fatalities, no progress will be made until police officers and civilians make personal progress within themselves enough to be willing to stand for what's right and denounce what's wrong no matter the skin color and with or without a uniform.

It is important to remember that being emotionally charged is not enough to endure the course that is necessary to produce permanent change. Move-ments start in a person that realizes that the time for being stagnated has come to an end. The thing that brings about cohesion is the participation of those that carry those same sentiments in heart. Visible progress comes as a result of an invisible process.

What about you? How long will you allow life to pass you by? You were born to make an impact now! If you continue to wait, now will become then and your moment in time will have moved on. What are you waiting for? Whatever your answer is, it's not good enough. The time has come to eliminate excuses and push forward toward your dreams.

This book was written to get you to move. You were not designed to be a monument. You were designed to be a movement. But, it must start within you. It's time for you and I to be powerful personal movements that partner together for progress. It doesn't matter the lane that you move in; business, academics, family, ministry, etc. The principles of making progress are universal. If you are going to move forward and make progress concerning the purpose and plan for your life, you must GO.

# INTRODUCTION

One of the worse things that can happen to anyone is to think we're going when in actuality, we're not. I call it running on life's treadmill. The interesting thing about "running on life's treadmill" is the amount of deception that comes with it. I mean… your feet are moving, you're sweating, you're out of breath, and you're probably losing weight if you're doing it on a consistent basis. The screen in front of you says that you've run X number of miles, but there's one major indicator that you haven't gone anywhere; the scenery hasn't changed. This, unfortunately, describes the life of so many people. They started off with high aspirations and expectations, and somewhere along the line they got satisfied with the activity, rather than productivity. Running on the treadmill is ok; if you just want to race against the clock…the clock being life. But, if you want to make progress, and move, and see something different, and experience different things – different terrains, different obstacles, different distances, and different levels of elevation – you will never accomplish those things running on life's treadmill. Now, I'm not knocking those of you that are running on the treadmill of life. It's a very convenient thing to do. Think about it: you're inside, you're protected from all of the natural elements, no rain or cold; you don't have all the discomforts that come with running from one location to the next. So it can be very tempting. The problem comes when the run becomes the rut; and you begin to feel stuck, stagnant, stiff, and stale, and now you're just going through the motions. Wake up in the morning, get the kids off to school, go to work, pick the kids up, come home, feed the dog, watch a little TV, go to bed, get up and do it all over again; that's the routine. Over time you become a moment chaser rather than a moment maker. You begin to say things like, "When I get out of school," or "When I get a job," "When I start a family," "Once the kids grow up," "When I retire"…I'm going to be able to do. And you look up and find out that the scenery has never changed, and you've been chasing moments rather than making them. If this sounds like you, then this book is right on time!

Mundane, mediocre, monotony was never God's intent for our life! He chose us, set us aside, then planted us in the earth so that we would move forward, reproduce and have a lasting impact *(John 15:15-16)*. It's time for you to GO!

# God Only

*"Live for an audience of one."*

# God Only

At the onset of this book there is a decision that must be made in order for you maintain a fixed focus. While all of us have people, things, and/or experiences that we tend to use as our driving force, when we don't place our dependency on something larger than life itself, our success becomes subject to the strength of whatever is supplying us with energy. In other words, whatever we allow to inflate us has also been given the right to deflate us. If it's the applause that energizes us, we'll find ourselves not running as strong when the applause is not there. If it is a person that makes us fight through challenges, if that relationship dissolves, we may have difficulty finding the tenacity to press through the pain.

If you are going to GO, you must have GOD ONLY as the definitive driving force. This is something that must be settled on the front end of your journey. It's what I like to call a righteous resolve. It simply means that if God is your dominant leader and He has insight concerning every facet of your days *(Psalm 31:15),* then the current sets of circumstances are not any that He is not aware of. With that in mind, the notion of losing becomes obsolete especially considering that He enjoys seeing you win *(Psalm 35:27, 2 Corinthians 2:14).*

It's amazing how many people divvy the dash. What do I mean? Well, on most headstones there is a birth date, and there is also a death date. In between the two is usually a dash. Everyone is born by themselves. Even if they are a twin, triplet or more, they were born separately. Everyone also dies by themselves. Even if they were in a massacre where many lost their lives, each person had to die for themselves. So, what about the dash? We're born ourselves. We have to die for ourselves. But, for some strange reason most "divvy the dash" in the middle to everyone else. We wear what people think is cool. We talk how others want us to talk. We drive vehicles and live in neighborhoods that others have defined as exclusive. Our preferences tend to be rooted in people, which can distract us from our purpose, which is rooted in God.

Now is the time for you to live your life for your creator. What does that mean? Does it mean to go to church all the time? Does it mean to pray and study more? Does it mean to become more religious? Those things are components of what this means. Simply put, living your life for God means using every day as another opportunity to fulfill the purpose and plan that God has for you. It is total submission to why you were born and allowing that to rule over yours' and others' opinions of what that looks like *(1 Peter 5:6)*.

## On The Go

GOD ONLY - Make a written assessment of the people and/or things in your life that are taking your attention away from God and his plan for you. Disconnect from everything on your list that is unnecessary or detrimental. If there are people on your list that you consider are permanent, ONLY engage in those relationships in the areas that are productive.

# Grand Outlook

*"The ability to see things properly and clearly are keys to you moving forward."*

# Grand Outlook

One of the qualities that is necessary to achieve anything substantial, especially God-sized, is the ability to time travel. Think for a moment. What is time for anyway? Time is a tool. It is good for measuring, monitoring, managing and maneuvering. It is NOT the determining factor for manifesting *(Mark 4:26-28)*.

If you are going to GO, you must have a GRAND OUTLOOK! The ability to see things properly and clearly are keys to you moving forward. This is called Vision. Vision gives you the ability to perceive as a reality God's original intent. You cannot trust your perspective enough to risk your success because your vantage point will always have blind spots. Whether looking into the past, present or future, individually none of them are strong enough to support the weight of your dream alone, but they can help. Here is what I mean.

Looking into the past, we can gain hindsight. Hindsight gives us the ability to harvest the fruit of the past. It helps us become better rather than bitter about situations that may not have seemed to be beneficial where our success is concerned. Get the lesson or be forced to repeat it. The only thing worse than going through is; going through, not getting the lesson, then going through it again. Don't just go through it, grow through it! Whether the past was painful or pleasant, it has the ability to serve as a point of reference to add value for your vision or dream.

Looking into the present, we can gain insight. Insight is the ability to maximize the moment. This is very important because maximized moments manufacturer momentum and maintained momentum makes movements. It helps us not to squander precious time that is designed to assist us. Whatever situation you may find yourself in now, I guarantee that there is a lesson to be learned for the next level. Kindergarten isn't for kindergarteners; it's for future first graders.

Looking into the future, we can gain foresight. Foresight allows us to project and plan. I know it's a cliché, but I'll say it anyway. If you fail to plan, plan to fail. Hindsight is great, insight is great as well, but to move forward it's not enough to know where you've come from or where you are. You must have some idea of where you're going. Even if you don't have all the details, a general sense of direction is mandatory. Without it, more harm than good can be done. You may find yourself in a quicksand-like situation and become more stuck than ever.

Be careful not to fall for the misconception that says, "Now is all that there is and all that there ever will be." That can be a fatal mistake because it provides opportunities for us to make very permanent decisions in situations that can be resolved with temporary solutions. This is how suicide becomes an option. I'm not just talking about physical death. Any type of self-sabotage can be considered suicidal. When people feel all hope is gone some commit financial suicide. They spend their savings or jump of the bridge into an ocean of debt. Some commit relational suicide. They burn bridges with people that have been placed in their lives to assist them in being better.

Never allow the past, present or projections to paralyze your progress. Yes, they can seem overwhelming if you don't view them in their proper tense and context. The past is behind you. The present will be the past tomorrow. The future is not here yet. So begin to look at the B.I.G., Best In God, picture knowing that your steps are ordered *(Psalm 37:23)* and that your life is a part of God's masterful plan *(Ephesians 2:10, Jeremiah 29:11)*.

## On The Go

It's time for a dreaming session. Take time to brainstorm and describe the big picture. If there were no limitations on your dream and you had unlimited resources, what would it look like? Write everything down that you can think of. Go find pictures that bring those words to life and place them in a place where you can see them regularly. This now becomes the representation and reference point of your dream *(Proverbs 28:19)*.

# Gage Opposition

*"Never confuse the enemy with the inner me."*

## Gage Opposition

Everything that is worth anything is prone to resistance. There haven't been any people that have had substantial success that have not had to fight for that success to be realized. Go ahead and settle that fact now! You will face opposition. Think about it, op-position. There will always be people, circumstances and events that seem to stand in the direct opposite position to the direction you're traveling. Sometimes it is deliberate. Sometimes it is not a malicious or intentional act. But, whether by design or by default, opposition is real!

If you're going to GO, you must GAGE OPPOSITION! Now that you know that opposing forces are waiting to ambush you as you go, it's important that you strategize and prepare for the attack. But, before we prepare for the next fight, let's take a look at how we lost the last one.

What was it that got you stuck? When did you lose the excitement of attaining your dream? Was it the face of adversity? Was it the unexpected children? Was it the layoff? What about financial issues? Did someone tell you that you are too old? Did you get sick? What was your opposition? Or should I ask what "IS" your opposition?

The lists of things that have the potential to stop us from moving forward are endless. We all could pick out great reasons why we haven't achieved. But, the truth is, every one of the things on those lists have one common denominator, us! Never confuse the enemy with the inner me.

It's amazing how much credit we give external conditions

where our success is concerned. But, in the same breath, we say, "Greater is he that is in me, than he that is in the world," (*1 John 4:4*). The devil is defeated remember *(James 4:7)*? So why is it that as the resistance against our dreams persists, we find ourselves becoming prisoners to our conditions and we schedule our release dates based on current situations and circumstances?

The reality is we have everything in us from birth to live our dreams. If we didn't have the tools for the job, but God required us to do the job anyway, God would be setting us up for failure. But, the fact that we know he delights in us winning *(Psalm 35:27)*, suggests that the tools are there whether we know it or not *(Jeremiah 1:5; 29:11)*. The terrain of life is the process that's designed to grow and groom us so that the purpose and plan of God are fulfilled *(Ephesians 2:10 AMPC)*. When we realize that nothing can stop us but us, gaging the opposition becomes completely an internal exercise. The question becomes, how are YOU preventing YOU from being the best YOU?

## On The Go

What are the triggers that activate internal resistance? Pray for God to give you a trusted accountability partners and identify your challenges then put strategic safeguards in place to protect you from you.

# Get Offensive

*"Winners must put points on the board."*

# Get Offensive

They say defense wins championships. I don't dispute that fact. Even though I haven't won a championship since my 6th grade middle school basketball team, I do know that no matter how much defense is played in any sport, the team that puts the most points on the board will ultimately be the winner. No winning team creates a "defense only" strategy. Progressive, forward thinkers that take timely action will win every time. If you are going to GO, you must GET OFFENSIVE!

Too many people that claim to want to live their dreams are sitting by waiting for their ship to come in. Wrong! While the ship is preparing to come in, you've got to be doing something that will cause you to maximize the ship's arrival. Then, if the ship continues to be delayed, that means it's time to go swimming and bring it in! What steps can you take NOW toward your dream being a reality?

I opened a barber and beauty salon years ago called Legendary Cuts. I was like most aspiring entrepreneurs. I was so eager to open this place, but I didn't have the money yet to fund the idea. So, I decided to get offensive. I didn't call it that at the time; I simply set out to do everything I could do to start the business that didn't cost any money. I spent countless hours at the library and online researching the market and industry trends. I began to study what areas would be most beneficial for me to offer services to the demographic I had chosen. I created a detailed business plan. I picked out all the furniture. I found out who had the best prices. I researched the contractors I wanted to use and got bids from them. I left no stone unturned. By the time I had a clear vision, the provision was there. I learned that money is not the answer to attaining your dream. The dream is already there. Money only acts as a channel to facilitate it materializing. For most people, it's the first thing we want, but it's usually the last thing we need. I say that because money without a clear vision becomes a waste by default. Why pay to learn the lessons that can be learned for free. Contrary to popular belief, patience is a key to being progressive. It allows us to think things through with detail and visit a variety of scenarios without having to incur the cost of being anxious. Haste makes waste! When you're on the offense, you ask questions, and you listen to learn because you are always looking for ways to be ahead of the game.

One of the most interesting things to me is when people tell me they desire to open a business. The first thing I typically ask is the name of the business. If they don't have a name, the conversation immediately shifts. I begin to talk to them about what I'm telling you now. The fact that they don't have a name says to me that they aren't really as serious as they are making themselves seem. Why? What does it cost to come up with a name? Better yet, why not have a few names to choose from?

Getting offensive is about putting points on the board by making every move count! The dream is yours. You have to make the call! Send the letter! Ask the questions!

Remember that not doing something is doing something. When we don't do anything, what we have done is postponed the reality of our dreams.

## On The Go

What have you been waiting on to come to you that you can go and get for yourself? For the next six weeks, do one thing each week that will put you one step closer to your dream. Next, for twenty-one (21) days straight, do one thing every day that will put you one step closer to your dream. Every time you miss a week or a day start over. No cheating!

# Gifts Operating

*"Gifts are God's investment in us. His Return On Investment comes through us."*

# Gifts Operating

Each person that is born into the earth has been given a unique set of tools that are designed to bring ease to their particular assignment. These tools are also known as gifts. Unfortunately, when many hear the word gift, we don't make the association with how they can be beneficial practically. That is a problem because if we don't see gifts as part of who we are all the time, we will compartmentalize them and put them on reserve for use during worship services and church events. The truth of the matter is gifts are supernatural endowments that have practical applications to accomplish many tasks. There are biblical accounts where men were gifted to build things with intricacy and elaborate detail. They were gifted by God, through the Holy Spirit to make artistic designs for work in gold, silver and bronze, to cut and set stones, to work in wood and to engage in all kinds of artistic crafts *(Exodus 35:30-33)*.

Some feel like looking at gifts from this perspective may not seem as glamorous as the word of knowledge, word of wisdom, working of miracles and the others that we most commonly refer to *(1 Corinthians 12)*. But, they are absolutely necessary in living your dream! If you're going to GO, you must have GIFTS OPERATING.

We would need an entirely separate book to talk about gifts in full details. What I hope to accomplish in this book is to give you enough insight about gifts to whet your appetite so that you begin to see the value in your giftedness, identify what your gifts are and put them to work toward living your dreams. God invested gifts in us and he is not a bad investor. He expects a Return On his Investment (ROI).

Let's look at gifts from a few perspectives:

## DESIGN

Before we were in our mother's womb we were designed for a specific purpose *(Jeremiah 1:5)*. We were handcrafted with tools so that we could be tools that are suitable for use to accomplish great exploits *(Ephesians 2:10, Daniel 11:32)*. Gifts are not earned. They are God-given advantages that have been given to us as being supernaturally part of our divine design.

## DISCOVERY

Gifts are not decided; they are discovered. Here is a very simple formula to discover gifts:

ASK – Ask God. He is the One that gave them to you. God does not want you to be without this information. He will highlight things that you may not be able to recognize on your own.

ASSESS – Assess what you have been prone to throughout your life. What things do you do well with little effort? What do people look to you for that they don't look to others for?

ACCEPT – Accept your gifts. Find and protect the value in being uniquely you. Don't fight the distinction that will be made between you and others. Your gifts are designed to make you stand out.

## DEVELOPMENT

Don't be fooled when you see gifts in full operation. If you are not careful, you might think that the gift that you are looking at has always been that way. Not at all! Whatever the area of gifting is; arts, entertainment, business, ministry, or otherwise, I guarantee that there was a process to reaching this point. Much like muscles, when we are born we have all the gifts we are going to have. Also, like muscles, when gifts go unused they have a tendency to weaken and deteriorate. Every gift, I repeat, every gift requires countless hours of being honed and perfected through purposeful practice. It is the practice process that refines our gifts enough for them to take us to our destiny.

## DIRECTION

Discovery and identification tend to have a way of automatically producing direction because in the process we find out what things are. But, simultaneously we find out what they are not. This is most valuable where are gifts are concerned because with a direction in mind we are able to prevent losing valuable time, energy and resources. Gifts act as a North Star that guides us toward the purpose and plan of God for our lives.

## DRIVE

We will always have more stick-to-itiveness in our area of gifting than we do in other areas. That doesn't mean we can't try new things. Some things are simply for enjoyment and recreation. But, the dream, the assignment, the vision that God has for our life, will require tireless persistence and drive that can only be accessed by using our gifts.

## On The Go

Take the time to look within to discover your divine design. What unique qualities do you possess that can move you toward your dreams? If you have trouble identifying seeing those things, gather a group of trusted friends or family members and ask them to describe the unique things about you. Use the information that you gather as a starting place to look at yourself more clearly.

G.O.

# Get Out

*"Exposure expands our expectations."*

# Get Out

This particular principle may seem rather obvious. It is absolutely understandable that you feel that way. It's blatantly clear that going requires movement. Just keep reading and I think you will discover the necessity of this part of the book. The power in this principle is found when we become aware that every level that we will reach must first be introduced to us before we get there. How we respond to the introduction will determine whether or not we can move in it. If you are going to GO, you must GET OUT!

One of the most powerful statements that I have ever heard was said to me by my mentor, Apostle Amos. L. Howard, Sr. He rocked my world when he said, "Exposure expands your expectations." Whoa! It was a revelation that allowed me to see God in the things that I would be exposed to.

Years ago, I made my living as a Master Barber. During that time I was blessed to have several professional athletes as clients. The more I serviced those clients, the more they gave me access to their personal lives. It was an amazing experience to see a multimillionaire, who was in his early twenties, spend thousands of dollars at one time. To see someone that you know personally drive cars that most people only saw their favorite celebrity drive on TV was eye-opening to say the least. At the time I had no clue what was happening. I just knew that I was enjoying the ride.

After several years had passed, I relocated six hundred miles from home and there I discovered my purpose. In doing so, I realized that God had set me up. He had allowed me to be exposed to that type of money for a few reasons. Number one, it showed me that people really lived like that. It lit a fire in me to have a higher quality of life. Number two, it made fantasy a reality. Because I was in that environment, it's very hard for me to be star-struck or impressed by material things. Don't get me wrong, I like nice things, but I'm not impressed. Thirdly, that season in my life taught me that money is only useful for goods and services. Those guys had some of the same issues as everyone else, and in some cases, the problems were worse. This was a key lesson for me because it took away the ability to be bought or to compromise for money.

God used that situation to expand my thinking without me knowing it. But, in hindsight, I don't believe that I was able to maximize this principle. It is very difficult to extract the lessons when the class is over. That's why I am sharing this with you. Maybe you don't have an Amos Howard to show you what the next level looks like by taking you under his/her wing. Maybe you haven't had an opportunity to roll with professional ball players. It's ok! You have the ability to intentionally connect to the next level on your own. We don't have to wait to be exposed to the next level. We can expose ourselves to people, places and things that will expand our ability to think bigger about what we expect out of life *(Proverbs 23:7)*. With the world at our fingertips through the Internet, we can literally go anywhere.

How does this principle work? Remember, exposure expands our expectation. Here are a few examples: I once aspired to buy a nice used car and make monthly payments. My expectation was expanded when I saw a person buy multiple luxury cars and trucks in cash! I once was impressed with certain brands of shoes until my expectation was expanded when I was exposed to people who wear them once before they trash them. I once thought that all men cheat. My expectation for my marriage was expanded when I was exposed to faithful family men that didn't cheat on their spouses. I once thought that money was the root of all evil until my expectation was expanded when I became exposed to good, integral people that loved God and were rich. I think you get my point.

The key to getting the fruit from this principle is how you respond at the point of exposure. If the next level provokes fear, jealousy, envy, lust, rage, bitterness, or anxiety this principle won't benefit you until you can overcome those emotions. Those emotions are opposed to God, and they are designed to keep you in a place that is beneath the level that you have been exposed to. Never allow negative emotions to determine your perspective of the next level or those who have arrived there before you. When this happened to the children of Israel, even God could not get them to the next level. Twelve of them were exposed to the beauty and abundance of the land. They brought back proof to expose the others but their negative emotional response caused them not to experience it for themselves. Only two saw the fruit of the land. They were the only two who entered.

See something new. Do something different. Provoke your mind to think higher. If there is a restaurant that you want to experience but it is too expensive for where you are financially, go there and order desert. That slice of pie may be more than what you have ever paid for pie, but you are not paying for the pie. You are paying for the experience. It's the feel, the smells, the sounds of the next level that will give you the expectation necessary to have this as your normal life.

It doesn't cost you anything to test drive your dream car or walk through your dream house, or sit in the lobby of the hotel of your dreams, or try on an outfit by an exclusive designer at your dream boutique. Access to your dream has been denied long enough. Expose yourself to the next level then watch how you go in as you get out!

## On The Go

Make a list of as many things as possible that you would like to experience at the next level of your life. Next, be intentional to experience the next level a minimum of one time per month by going to places that you aspire to experience. Next, contact people who are where you desire to be. Offer to take them to lunch or dinner or find something that is unique to give them that they value. This is a great gesture to show them that you aren't looking for a handout.

TYMETRIC DILLON

# Glean & Observe

*"Learn to extract the **GO**ld."*

## Glean & Observe

Those who know me at all know that I am a big biopic interview buff. Some people consider those things boring, but for me, it is one of the most exciting things ever. For me, it is literally an opportunity to mine the minds of people. The difference between people like me and those that are bored with the biopics and interviews is the ability to extract gold. I consider myself a life-long learner, so whether it is a rapper, a preacher, a musician or a businessman, I can learn the principles of success because they are universal. In actuality, whether they are successful or unsuccessful, they all have something that they can teach me. Sometimes the lesson is what not to do! In my opinion, experience is not the best teacher. If it is, I don't have to be the one to experience it to get the lesson. If you are going to GO, you must GLEAN & OBSERVE.

Gleaning is a word that is not used too much these days. But it couldn't be more important at any other time than it is now. What is it exactly? Gleaning has to do with extracting, gathering and/or obtaining. Why is this important? This is the way we press the gas on progress. When we see others operating in a way that is conducive to living out God's purpose and plan for our lives, we can advance further more quickly by extracting those habits and patterns that we see *(Hebrews 6:12)*.

Gleaning is like looking in a mirror. What do I mean? The purpose of a mirror is to use what is observed to make adjustments. Not just any adjustments. Mirrors should be used to make the appropriate adjustment. If someone looked in the mirror and saw that they needed to comb their hair but instead they washed their face that would not be the proper adjustment.

If they saw a stain on their shirt, but they changed their pants it wouldn't help them.

Gleaning and observing is the way we can watch carefully, and then extract the things that are necessary for our life. Getting this principle provides an opportunity for limitless learning. Things like live access tools and apps, give us unprecedented access to a world of expert teachers and mentors all across the globe that we can interact with.

Whether by default or by design we all are being offered information at a tremendous rate audibly and visually. It's up to us to do what prior generations called, "eating the meat and spitting out the bones". In other words, take what is useful and disregard the things that are not beneficial.

## On The Go

Begin to journal. Take 5 minutes or more each day to capture the significant moments on paper. Look into those moments as a mirror to make the appropriate adjustments that are necessary to move toward your dreams.

# Goodbye Obvious

*"Obvious is what's readily available not what's really available."*

# Goodbye Obvious

Most people put a lot of stock in having common sense. But, the only problem with that is, if that type of sense is what we aspire to have; we are aspiring to achieve commonality. If it's common, then it's not unique. It's not different. It doesn't stand out. Your days of being regular must end now!

If you're going to GO, you must say GOODBYE OBVIOUS. Sense reasoning without the Holy Spirit is death *(Romans 8:6)*. In other words, to just measure and judge things based on our human ability or to process information based on our limited thought patterns will not produce the type of results that God desires. We need something that's going to allow us to see what others can't see; which then positions us to do something that others can't do. Think about it: if success was so easy, everybody would have it. But on the other hand, the principles of success are easily and readily available. In this information age anything that we don't know is unknown only because we don't want to know. We don't have to go to the library any longer and do massive amounts of research. Instead, right on our mobile devices we can find anything we want to find. With the information about being successful being so accessible, why isn't everybody successful? I believe the reason is because many people are stuck on the obvious. It takes looking beyond what you can see with your natural eye to take the principles and transform them into a practical, pliable, application for the path that you're set on. In other words, knowing what to do with the information is just as important as the information itself. And it takes looking beyond what's right before us in order to get the desired result.

One of the most common phrases that we use when referring to those who are great and those who have really made great strides is, "They were ahead of their time." I think God is very intentional about the time we are born. I don't think any of us are born outside of the time that we're supposed to be born. God told Jeremiah that he knew him before he was inside his mother *(Jeremiah 1:5)*. So, that statement is not necessarily the most truthful statement. But, I do believe that those persons were able to see well beyond their time. Seeing beyond the obvious gives us the ability to extract the gold and leave behind those things which aren't beneficial toward our journey. It allows us to have insight so that we recognize the moment that we're in so that we maximize those moments. Moments that are maximized make momentum.

We have to say goodbye to obvious because the obvious is what's readily available not what's really available.

Let's use a smart phone for example. If we limited a smart phone to its "obvious" use we would never experience the benefit of many of the great things that it has to offer. Only those that are able to see that the smart phone is really a smart device that is capable of photography and video production with editing tools, administrative assistance, telecommunication, gaming center, music studio and music collection storage, health monitor, compass, calendar, and clock, will maximize what is possible.

What can be seen with the natural eye is not all that there is. Now is the time to start looking at what can only be seen through the eyes of your dreams *(2 Corinthians 4:18)*. What is really possible for you? Can you see it? Remember, we can only become what we are able to behold.

## On The Go

Dreaming takes practice. Start by taking 5 minutes each day to allow your limitless and creative imagination to operate uninterrupted. Be sure to document the things that you see. Once you've mastered 5 minutes, add time in increments of 5 minutes until you spend 1 hour each day focused on your dream. It's ok to dream the same dream multiple times!

G.O.

# Goals and Objectives

*"Goals don't have to be massive; but they do have to be measurable."*

## Goals & Objectives

One of the reasons some people never get 'there' is because in many cases they have no clue of what 'there' looks like. The destination is a vital piece of information because it provides us with directions. Even if we don't have concise, detailed instructions, we need some sense of where we are headed. Sometimes we get it as we go *(Luke 17:14)*. Without it we may not recognize when we're on the path to somewhere else.

If you're going to GO, you must have GOALS and OBJECTIVES. Goals & objectives are the pathways to completion. Without them, we can be misguided and misdirected. The other danger of not having goals and objectives is that you can tire more easily because you may have no sense of accomplishment. Without goals & objectives, you leave your dream to chance, and you're going after it through the method of trial and error…mostly error. Goals don't have to be massive; but, they do have to be measurable. They need to be something that can be assessed to say "yes, I've accomplished it." You don't want to say, "My goal is to have a good time." Well, what does a good time look like? To some, a good time is a bad time. How do you know if the goal was accomplished? How can you measure that? Are you expecting the experience to provoke a particular emotion or feeling? Goals should be something that's clear. Asking yourself questions can help make them clear. Who, what, when, where and why are great places to start. The answers to these questions are vital in setting measurable goals.

Objectives represent the purpose of the goals. This line of thinking is all throughout the Bible. I'm not sure why some believers haven't fully grasped it. We see things like "putting things behind us…pressing toward the mark" *(Philippians 3:13)*… that's a goal. "Looking unto Jesus the author and finisher of our faith" *(Hebrews 12:2)*. Even Jesus had goals and objectives. He said, "I've come that you might have life and have it more abundantly" *(John 10:10)*. That was the objective that he desired to accomplish as a result of coming to the earth. But here's the challenge with goals & objectives: they're not automatic. They must be executed. They must be put into practice if they're going to do what they're designed to do. Execution is the key. Remember this as you read this book: you can read this book from cover to cover, time after time, and still never "GO". Why? Any area that you're not willing to execute is the same area that you're not willing to experience.

## On The Go

    List 3 goals and objectives that you plan to accomplish within the next 12 months. If you complete a goal before the allotted time, replace it with a new goal.

# Grammatical Oneness

*"Only say what you want to see in your life."*

# Grammatical Oneness

Have you ever been playing around as a kid and someone said something that you didn't want to happen? Your response may have been something like, "Don't jinx me," or "I'm going to tell on you for calling me that." What were we really communicating? We were saying that we have an understanding, at some level, that what we say matters. Life and death are in the power of our tongue *(Proverbs 18:21)*. The realization of our dreams is hinged on what we say.

If we're going to GO, we must have GRAMMATICAL ONENESS. When it comes to speaking life or death, we have a choice. We have options in front of us. We have the option to say things that we desire to happen, but we also have the option to say what we do not desire to happen *(Deuteronomy 30:19)*. Somewhere along the line someone came up with the phrase "speaking things into existence". I understand what the phrase is attempting to communicate, but I also understand that as a Believer, that statement is not the most accurate phrase. I do agree with the phrase in the sense that we have the power to call those things that are not as though they were *(Romans 4:17)*. But, what we have to realize is, because they are not, that does not mean they don't exist. When we search the Scriptures a little more carefully, what we find out is that in all of creation everything was created, both visible and invisible *(Colossians 1:16)*. So in actuality, everything already exists. When we're calling things, we're not calling them into existence; we're calling them into our experience. Calling simply means summonsing them, or placing a demand on its presence. You know like jury duty. When you're summonsed to jury duty, you really don't have an option whether or not you're going to show up. You really don't have an opportunity to plead your case or tell why you can't make it. You're not given a form asking the most convenient time that you're available to serve. You're summonsed and not showing up provides for you a particular result. That's the type of attitude we have to have when it comes to our words. We have to call things into our experience. They already exist; whether or not we can see them really doesn't matter.

Remember that words create or cancel. Allow this principle to create consistency in your communication. Begin to speak one way. Only say the things that you desire to see. Begin to say things that are going to push you towards your goals and objectives; things that are going to push you toward attaining the dream that you have. Begin to speak life. Allow your mouth to be the thing that causes your miracle. Allow your mouth to be the thing that causes your manifestation. Allow your mouth to be the thing that releases what you desire to receive.

## On The Go

Write out a positive confession that reflects what you desire to have happen in your life. Make this confession a part of your daily speech.

# Guided Optics

*"We become what we behold!"*

# Guided Optics

This is another key chapter that's going to help you GO. If the blind lead the blind, they'll both end up in a ditch *(Matthew 15:14)*. We become what we behold!

So, if we're going to GO, we have to have GUIDED OPTICS. We have to see things from a particular vantage point that acts as a guide along the paths that have been predestined and prearranged for our lives *(Ephesians 2:10)*. We need laser like focus if we're going to be successful because lack of focus is designed to bring about instabilities. Distractions come to detour and derail our destinies. How does that happen? A double minded man is unstable in all his ways *(James 1:8)*. The eye of the body is light. If the eye be single, it will be full of light. But if not, then how great will the darkness be *(Matthew 6:22-23)*. So it's important that we have a guided point of view; that we're locked into where we're headed. Doing this has a way of making us stable and able to filter the things that desire to steal our time, our energy, our money, and our influence. These are some of the things that happen as a result of being distracted.

I remember when I opened my first business. I was so excited about the business, and I really wanted to serve everybody. I don't think it was a bad thing to want to service a large population, but I didn't take the time to narrow my focus at the beginning. I never took the time to assess the group I wanted to service, and anything outside that group would be an added bonus. One day, someone came in with an advertising opportunity in a magazine that, according to their numbers, my business would reach approximately 15,000 – 20,000 households. Right away, because I was new in business and wanted to be in front of as many people as possible, so 15,000 – 20,000 sounded wonderful to me. The way I figured it is hey, if only 1% of those people came to my business that would be 200 extra customers to patronize my business. Sounded good to me! It wasn't until I purchased the space in the magazine that I realized that yes, this magazine might have reached 20,000 households, but those 20,000 were not the demographic that I served. So, even if those 200 people came to my business, I couldn't service them. It would've been counterproductive to the growth of the business.

Whose fault was it? Was it the magazine company's fault? No, they were doing their job selling ads. Was it the customers' fault? No, the customers only wanted to be serviced. The issue was I didn't have anything to guide my vision. Therefore, I was looking all over the place and I got stuck on the numbers rather than the desired result. Learn from my mistake. Lock in and recognize what the dream looks like. Then stay focused on doing what's necessary to achieve the results. Yes, distractions will come. Some of them will even come disguised as great opportunities. But the way that you'll be able to make the distinction between what is just good, and what is God, is you're going to have to have a fixed focus so that making the judgment call is based on what you see in your heart. Protect that picture of what it looks like for you. Anything that does not match that, it's a distraction.

## On The Go

Images can serve as reminders of the vision that we have in our hearts. Create a constant reminder by placing pictures and/or words in your home, on phone or computer screen savers, or in any other places that you frequent. Only use those pictures and words that represent your vision. Be intentional to view it as often as possible.

# Guard Openings

*"Guard your heart; it determines the course of your life."*

## Guard Openings

In a previous chapter I talked about knowing what that picture looks like that's in your heart. When I talk about the heart, I'm not just talking about the thing that's in your chest that causes blood to flow through your body. I'm talking about the core of who you are. I'm talking about the very essence of your being. And that heart on the inside of you, that core, it's not just there for decoration, but it's a manufacturing center and it has the ability to produce whatever you put in. That's why I believe that we live life from the inside out. What's in our heart is the very thing that we're experiencing now. I'm writing this book because it's in my heart. I believe that these keys will help you move further. So the question becomes: how did what's in my heart get there? We have these openings, these gates, and they lead directly to our heart, again, which is the manufacturing center that is designed to produce what we put in, whether good or bad. If we are going to GO, we must GUARD OPENINGS.

One opening we have is our mouth. In speaking right things or speaking wrong things they both go through our ears, which is another opening, and it leads to our heart. We have the option to decide whether or not the heart, ear, and mouth connection will be a victorious or a vicious cycle. Here's how this works! Our words are invisible forces that have the ability to cause ships of circumstance to set sail at our command. They literally set the course for our lives. But, where do those words originate? They come from the heart *(Matthew 12:34)*. Out of the abundance of the heart the mouth speaks. So, if the heart is not guarded against destructive influences, it will produce a destructive language that will take on the form of word power. Those words then reinforce the destructive belief as we hear them when they are released through the mouth and the cycle continues. On the contrary, the opposite is true. If we allow constructive influences in our hearts, it will produce a constructive language that will take on the form of word power. Those words then reinforce the constructive belief as we hear them when they are released through the mouth, and the cycle continues.

The other opening that we must guard is our eyes – the things we see. These things have great influence on our heart. Our heart has great influence on what our lives look like. So if we're going to GO, we must guard openings. Guard the heart, for out of it flows the issues of life *(Proverbs 4:23)*. What does that really mean? One translation says to guard your heart because it determines the course for your life (NLT). I think that translation gives much clearer insight on what that means. We have the ability to shape our lives. We have the ability to sow things on the ground of our heart and those seeds will produce for us. Both of those translations have one word that is key in what I am attempting to tell you; LIFE. If I'm correct, most of us are alive 24/7/365. I don't believe that too many of us take breaks from life. That usually doesn't work out too well. The same way that we don't take a break from living, if we're going to guard our life by guarding the openings, we don't really have the option to take breaks from opening ourselves to things that will be counterproductive. What do I mean? This is an interesting principle, but it's very practical. Something as simple as allowing certain types of music into our ear opening causes us to feel a certain way, whether it's happy, sad, angry or excited. Certain types of songs can cause us to get a speeding ticket because it has us so excited that we can feel the force that comes from that music and it's played out in our life. What about through our eyes? There are certain things that we see, whether it's experienced live or we see it on TV, those types of images have a way of creating certain feelings. They say a picture is worth a thousand words. How much more is a video that contains millions of pictures combined to make movement. When we subject ourselves to seeing these things, slowly but surely, it's going to be played out in our lives. Let's use fashion for instance. Have you ever asked yourself why do I dress this way? It's probably something you've seen or heard "this is the latest thing". Most of us are influenced by what we've seen.

Those are small examples of how things enter into our heart. If we don't guard our openings they will take our lives on a course that we didn't plan for. The awesome thing is the opposite is true as well. If we intentionally put good things in our openings, if we put things in our ears that are going to keep us charged, that's going to give us encouragement, that's going to give us the stamina to stay the course long enough to attain the dream, that's great. If we see others who have crossed the finish line, accomplished similar goals, or any goals for that matter, it sends a signal to your heart that says "we can do this".

## On The Go

Take one week to begin to retrain your heart by not complaining, not listening to anything negative and not watching anything that you don't want to experience. Every time you violate one of these things you must start counting the week over again.

# Grade Opinions

*"Don't allow anyone to have automatic placement in your circle of influence."*

# Grade Opinions

It's amazing the people we give the opportunity to influence our lives. Most of them are close to us. That's what gives them the influence that they have. Only those that are close to us can touch the heart. We use all type of random criteria to justify people having the ability to shape our lives. Sometimes it's because people are SMART. We feel that because they have earned college degrees, they have insight intellectually so they have the right to occupy a certain space in our lives. Maybe it is because they're SPIRITUAL. We give them a place to dictate what our lives should look like because they seem to have a certain level of connection to God. Unfortunately, sometimes their opinions override the opinion of God Himself. Maybe it is because they have SUBSTANCE. Yeah, that's it! They have money and expensive things so they must know all the answers. Wrong! What about if they're SENSITIVE? They understand me; they get me; they empathize with me so maybe they should have a voice in how I live my life. Maybe it's their SECURITY that draws you in. They are secure in areas that you have insecurities, so you give them a certain place to compensate for what you see lacking within yourself. Oh, here's one for you: maybe they're SEXY. So, because of their appearance and because your hormones are busy, you allow this person to maneuver and manipulate you into doing what they think you should do. If you're going to GO, you must GRADE OPINIONS.

Think about it: something as simple as eating a good steak, ground beef, or chicken gives you insight on the value of Grade A. You never go into the meat section of a store and say, "This is Grade F meat and it's exactly what I want." We've never done that. So why don't you grade other things that you consume;

such as people's opinions? Why do you allow people who are performing at an "F" level in the relationship to have a Grade "A" opinion in your life? When you do, it's even more detrimental than eating bad meat because you consume these opinions in your thoughts and emotions and this adversely affects the course of your life *(Proverbs 23:7)*. This principle is a tough one because it forces you to categorize people by adding and subtracting value where opinions are concerned. It begins to separate people based on their qualifications to counsel you toward your dreams. In other words, titles don't give anyone the right to speak into your life nor should people automatically have a voice because of biological connection.

How do you grade people's opinions? Do they have a love for God? Do they have a love for you? Do they genuinely want to see you do well? What are their motives? How much do they know about the subject? Is it just an emotional thing, or are they really giving you sound advice? These are some of the concerns that must be addressed in order to grade properly. Don't allow anyone to have automatic placement in your circle of influence. But here's the key: do not base their grade on your level of comfort. It is not a matter of whether or not their opinion feels good, or it's something you want to hear. You must grade them on the scale of truth. Is what they're saying to you true? Is it the best thing for you to do, even if you don't want to do it? You must have strong, solid opinions if you're going to move forward and if you're going to GO.

## On The Go

Ask yourself a few questions. Who voice has influence in your decision-making? Why? If the people you have named don't meet the criteria for a passing grade, stop consuming their opinions.

G.O.

# Genuine and Official

*"Nobody can beat you being you!"*

## Genuine & Official

I came up in an era where there were a lot of single parent homes and mine was one of them. With that dynamic, it brought about some different issues and circumstances, one of them being the inability to stay current with the fashion trends. At one point, leather coats were the desired garments of choice. If you had a genuine leather coat, you were making a massive fashion statement and a statement about what your family could afford. The leather coat craze became so big that there was a great influx of fake leather coats. We called them "pleather" because they were plastic but designed to look like leather. People who bought those coats were mostly those that didn't understand authenticity. For those who wanted to be seen as prosperous, it was not enough to have a leather coat; you needed to have a genuine leather coat. One of the crazy ways people would determine if your coat was real was to smell them. The smell of leather would be the determining factor in the neighborhood as to whether or not your coat was authentic. Even before the smell test, there would be tags on the coat from the manufacturer that read, "Genuine Leather." Why? People who were looking for leather did not want to mistakenly buy a fake. There was something about having the real deal.

If you are going to GO, you must be GENUINE and OFFICIAL. This seems pretty simple, but the interesting thing is we live in a time where phony is preferred. You may not think so but look at devices such as your cell phones or tablets. Take a look at the "apps" and filters. Look at all of the ways that you can superimpose your image into a location that you have never been to. With today's technology, you can almost be whoever you would like to be, or you can present yourself as being someone other than your true self. Most people, through their smart device, have the capability to support that. What about something as simple as beauty supplies? I have never seen so many wigs and weaves. Fake hair is almost the new real hair. Who wears their real hair anymore? What about the makeup? It is not just the eyeliner, lipstick and a little blush here. It is extreme! It is at an entirely different level than it was years ago. Some even go to further extremities with getting new body parts. I will spare you the details on what those parts are, but you know what they are. There are so many people who are not satisfied with what God has given them anatomically, so they go to the plastic surgeon to rearrange a few things. Those are just a few examples, and they are based on physical traits and characteristics. What about how we mask the different areas of our lives to put on this facade of who we desire to be rather than who we really are? Now, it is important for you to know that I do understand the importance of imaging and imagining—seeing yourself at a different level than you may be currently. I believe that we can foresee things and we can begin to project our minds further than our current situations or circumstances. That is not what I am talking about. I am talking about when we begin to hide and to mask the real us. Let's use the makeup example again. In my personal opinion, there is nothing wrong with makeup. I believe the problem comes when the makeup is utilized for something more than just for beauty purposes…more than just for the aesthetics or the appearance, but it becomes something to hide and to literally conceal something that is designed to deceive individuals to think that you are not who you really are. When you begin to become so dependent on that to where you don't feel like yourself without it, then I believe that is an issue.

What about hair? What is wrong with curly hair? What is wrong with coarse hair? Yes, it may require a different level of care to manage, but there is nothing wrong with it. There is no such thing as "bad" hair. But when our minds have been conditioned to a particular thing, it has the ability to become a problem. It begins to devalue those who don't have those particular characteristics. Being genuine and official simply put is an invitation to be the real you. Are you being the real you? The answer is in the "Why?" Why do you do the things that you do? Why do you dress the way that you dress? Why do you live in the neighborhood that you live in? Is it a place where you really want to be or is it a place to bring value to how others see you? Is it something where you are trying to make others feel that you are somebody and that you have everything together? Do you drive that kind of car because it is a status symbol and you want people to think that you have arrived? So many people are doing so many things that are just not them. They marry into families that do not represent their values and what they believe. They take jobs and follow career paths that they don't find fulfillment in. There are so many things that we all do because of the opinions of other people.

What if we were able to get back to the real us? I'll tell you what would happen. You would expedite your success because that is the sweet spot. That is the place where you have been created to be. That is the lane that you have been created to flow in. In that place you will find fulfillment, you will find enjoyment. You will find everything that you need because it is who you have been purposed to be. Think about it. We hear the story of The Prodigal Son and how he left his father's house and started acting wild and crazy. He returned to his father's house and his father welcomed him after doing all of those crazy things. One of the key points of that story is that he had an introspective moment. He had a moment where "he came to himself." After coming to himself, to who he really was, it was at that point he could return and go back to the place of prosperity, the place of protection, the place of provision *(Luke 15:11-24)*.

There are so many things that are pulling you away from you—the media, friends and family members, and culture and these things are telling us to follow the path that everyone else is following. As a result, there is a traffic jam, because everybody is trying to go in the same direction. But if you are going to GO, you must be genuine and official. Sometimes you have to go against the grain, and that's okay. As long as you are following the path that God has purposed and planned for your life, you will be fine. Nobody can be you, except you. Nobody can beat you being you!

## On The Go

If there is an area in your life that you don't want others to know the truth about, get rid of it. ANYTHING that is not authentically you must go. Being exposed could be detrimental to your reputation and counterproductive to living your dream.

# Gather Others

*"No team, no dream!"*

# Gather Others

I am sure that you have heard it said that no man is an island. The Bible says that two are better than one *(Ecclesiastes 4:9)* — one can put a thousand to flight; two can put ten thousand to flight *(Deuteronomy 32:30)*. I like to say it this way, "No team, no dream!" There is something about having the right connections. The right network allows us to work the net. It is great to fish with a single pole, but there is nothing like having that net there if you desire to grab a massive amount of fish. Whether your fish are clients, customers, patrons, members, friends or dollars, you're going to need a network to live out your dreams. If you are going to GO, you must GATHER OTHERS.

It is important to understand that gathering others does not mean that we are randomly giving out open invitations for sporadic individuals to participate in the journey to attaining our dream. That is not what this is. God arranges the body as He sees fit *(1 Corinthians 12:18)*. Gathering is a very specific and strategic selection of those individuals who would act as assets toward the fulfillment of the purpose and plan for your life.

The word "gather" in and of itself is an agricultural type of word. I think about fruit and vegetables when I'm thinking about gathering. Maybe it's my childhood summers in Louisiana, but I believe that when we gather others, when we gather people that are going to benefit us, people that are going to assist us in fulfilling our dreams, we can't just go for the low hanging fruit. When we pick the fruit, we have to be very good fruit inspectors because sometimes the fruit is rotting. Sometimes it is good fruit, but it isn't ripe yet. It is not ready to be picked. Sometimes the fruit has already fallen to the ground, but it is good fruit and it is up to us to pick it up and clean it off.

All of those scenarios are very realistic possibilities when it comes to gathering others. Characteristics of people—their integrity, their character, their intentions—all of those things are the components that we use to measure whether or not that fruit is ripe and ready. If it is ripe and ready, then we have to do what is necessary to gather it. Get a ladder. Get up there and get that fruit. Bend over, get down on the ground, pick up that fruit, clean it and use it for what it is needed for. Whatever can be done, within the context of good character and integrity, to gather the ripe, ready fruit, go for it! Whatever you do, do not just sit by and wait for the fruit to come to you.

It would be weird for a farmer or a person that is managing an orchard to sit by in their nice, comfortable rocking chair waiting for the fruit to put itself in the basket, meet them on the porch and say, "Hey, we're ready for you to use us!" That's typically not how this works. It even sounds a little strange. The same thing happens with people. We interact with different individuals daily. Some of those individuals have what we need to help us go to the next level. Your GIFTING requires LIFTING! Who's helping you get your BIG dreams off of the ground? The people in your life are either PUSHING YOU UP or PULLING YOU DOWN! There is no in between. Never underestimate the power of RIGHT relationships.

However, be careful not to measure the value of the relationship based on whether or not the person reciprocates the pursuit. This key is vital to you moving toward your dreams. Everyone wants to be pursued, but there are not a lot of people that desire to do the pursuing. Don't be like those people. You need to find the person who is doing what you desire to do and make every effort to connect with them. Find the person who has the information that you need to GO the next level and then do what it takes to get that information or develop that relationship. They have what you need! I call these types of individuals gatekeepers. They have the capability of determining who will come in and out of a particular circle or environment. When you have these types of individuals on your team, when you have favor with them and a listening ear, it is better than picking ripe fruit. It's like picking the whole tree, if that were possible. Having influence with the key players is beneficial because it gives you credibility with others that may be able to assist you.

In gathering others, in putting together your team, have patience. Be strategic. Assess where the gaps are, those areas where you need assistance; where you may not be as efficient or effective as you desire to be, or need to be. Find people who bring strength and wholeness to the team that you are putting together. Here's a clue for you: Just because they are strong, it does not mean that their strength should override and have more value than yours. Don't allow someone who is a strong part of your team to become the team. This is your dream. This is what you have been assigned to do. Stay in the driver's seat as you gather others.

## On The Go

Create a list of those that are currently on your team and what their roles and responsibilities are. Rank them on a scale of 1 to 10 with 1 being poor performance and 10 being an excellent performance. Consider dismissing everyone performing below 5. PLEASE keep in mind that each assessment might be based on different criteria. Each team member should serve a purpose. Some contributions are tangible, and others are not. Whether it is hard skills, innovation, creativity, team unity, emotional support, or other resources, be sure to judge their value appropriately. Meet with the remaining team to ensure that everyone is clear about the position they hold. Then give them a realistic period of time to perform consistently at an 8 or higher or meet the same fate as their former team members. Create another list of the roles and responsibilities that still need to be managed by someone. Set your sights on those people that can add value. Go after the missing pieces.

G.O.

# Gag Offense

*"TAKING offense requires GIVING joy, peace, and promotion in exchange."*

# Gag Offense

As you gather this team, you will discover that as talented as they are individually, getting them to utilize that talent in a cohesive manner that benefits the team can be a completely different thing. You are going to have all types of personalities, all types of backgrounds, and all types of perspectives. Yes, the vision may be the same, but there is something about our humanity and our interaction with one another that requires us to be intentional about how we operate. If we just go about it haphazardly, we will allow the small foxes to come and to spoil the vine *(Song of Solomon 2:15)* —the very thing that we're working so hard towards. Something as simple as someone's preference will get our eyes off of the purpose of us being together in the first place. We see it happening a lot in marriages and other relationships that are designed to accomplish things together. It's called being offended. If you're going to GO, you must GAG OFFENSE.

Offense has no place in your success. It has no place in your dreams, not even a little bit. Offense is a type of seed that comes in to bring about a hardened heart. It comes in through so many ways, whether it's through an argument, a difference of perspective, or sensitivity to a past hurt or pain. It comes in through a multiplicity of ways, but one of the things that all offended people have in common is that they "took" offense.

Think about that statement; take offense. It says to me two things: First, I have some control in the matter when it comes to whether or not I will be offended. Offense cannot invade my space unless I choose to "take" it. That means that no one can offend me. The only thing that they can do is offer me the opportunity to take it. If I choose not to sign for the package, then I don't have to be offended. The second thing that taking offense says to me is that if I am going to take offense, what am I going to release out of my hands to take it? Think about if you take something with your physical hands. If you already have something in your hands, how can you take what is being offered to you unless you set aside what you have in your hands? In the situation where being offended is concerned, typically an exchange is made. It is similar to a currency exchange. We have to give something to get something. In most cases, being offended costs us the exchange of our joy, our peace, our innovativeness, our tenacity, our stamina, our resilience, our motivation, our momentum our creativity. It costs us numerous amounts of positive things in exchange for this one negative, dream-crushing, thing. Why do people make the exchange? Well, being offended can feel amazing. Holding a grudge can feel like the right thing to do. If you are reading this book, you are probably a go-getter, or at least you desire to be one. There is something about being a go-getter that has an "I'm not weak" type of quality to it. Part of what we do on a regular basis is conflict resolution, and that is never easy. When someone backs us against the wall, we don't want to be seen as weak even if it means that we become overly aggressive in an attempt to prove our strength. In actuality, it is really a matter of pride. This is dangerous to our dreams because pride can be detrimental and destructive. Pride always precedes destruction and haughtiness comes before a fall *(Proverbs 16:18)*. It can cause things to be stopped up, to be stagnant and to stop flowing. An offended man is like a fortified city *(Proverbs 18:19)*. There is nothing coming in, and there is nothing going out. It is a place of stagnation. That is why we have to gag offense. We have to suffocate it and take the life away from it. We cannot just put it to the side to be dealt with at a later date. We have to attack it with vengeance, and we cannot be satisfied until the offense lies lifelessly by as we step over it on the path to our success.

## On The Go

Call everyone that has offended you and forgive him or her. If you have done the offending, ask them for forgiveness. Then forgive yourself! Move on!

*G.O.*

# Grow Older

*"Destinations are determined by maturation."*

# Grow Older

We are in the seventeenth chapter now and I hope you have noticed that each chapter title has been alliterated with "GO", so it reminds us to GO. We could have called this chapter, Get Older, but I think it is important for you to get what I am trying to communicate to you. We have to continue to grow older, not just get older. There is a process that you and I must go through if we are going to mature. I believe that the only thing that is worse than going through an uncomfortable phase in life is to go through that phase and not get the lesson. There are so many people who are aging chronologically and biologically, but emotionally, psychologically, mentally and financially, their development has been arrested. If you are going to GO, you must GROW OLDER.

I once worked with a young lady who shared with me that her husband seemed to stop maturing around their early twenties. She talked about how life had begun to move on, yet he stayed the same. He dressed the same; his interests were the same. He enjoyed video games and still carried himself as if he was that young guy who had zero responsibilities. The situation had gotten so bad that she and the children lived in one part of the house while her husband occupied an entirely different area of the house. The more she talked, the more I began to get an understanding of what was going on. I found out that this young man's mother had passed away in his early twenties and the grief was unbearable, so much so that it caused him to stop developing mentally and emotionally. It caused his growth to be stunted. He and his mother were so close that when she died a part of him did too.

There are so many like that young man. It might not have been the death of a loved one, but it may have been getting fired from a job, not getting the promotion, vehicle repossession or foreclosure. It may have been having children unexpectedly at an early age. It may have been sickness or disease that came around out of the blue. What about divorce? That may have the ability to stunt one's growth. All of these things have the ability to cause us to stop moving forward. However, it is up to us to decide whether these moments in life will be stepping stones or tombstones. The choice is ours.

Even though we are heirs of God and we are co-heirs with Jesus Christ *(Romans 8:17)*; even though we have been tremendously blessed with everything we need for life and godliness *(2 Peter 3:1)*, it totally depends on whether or not we mature. Even though we are heirs, as long as the heir is a child, he is no more than a slave, though he be lord of all *(Galatians 4:1)*. It would be no different than if I were to give my daughter, who is five-years-old at the time I am writing this book, the opportunity to drive in my lap as we pull up the truck in the driveway. She thinks she is really driving, but she is not mature enough to understand the dangers or the responsibilities of being a person on the road behind the wheel of a motored vehicle. Right now in her five year old mind, she is doing everything that is necessary to get the job done. Can you imagine me giving her my keys and saying, "Honey, enjoy yourself! Take Daddy's truck and do whatever you like!" That would be foolish. It would bring harm to her and others, not to mention her mother and me if something were to happen to her. The same is the case when it comes to our Heavenly Father. He is not going to do anything to bring harm to us or allow us to bring harm to ourselves *(Luke 11:11-13)*. We must mature.

Interesting enough, this requirement was the same even for Jesus Christ, the Messiah. The Savior of the world grew in wisdom and He grew in stature *(Luke 2:52)*. He matured. It is time for you to grow older emotionally. There is no way that you are going to attain or maintain the dream, the vision, the assignment that God has given to you if you are always on an emotional roller coaster. You have to grow older. You have to grow older psychologically. You have to think through things differently than you would have in your younger years before you had the experiences that you have. You have to grow older mentally. You have to learn mental toughness if you are going to experience what the plan of God is; the purpose for your life. No one can do this for you; you have to do this for yourself. When I was a child, I thought as a child. I spoke as a child. I did childish things. But when I became a man, when I matured, "I" put away the childish things *(1 Corinthians 13:11)*. Now don't get me wrong, your Father will assist you and help you by His Spirit, but you must make the step and have the desire to grow and to mature in every area of your life. Your manifestation hinges upon your maturation. Grow up!

## On The Go

Take a long, hard look at your life. Identify the undeveloped and/or underdeveloped areas. Find people who are developed in each of those areas that you are not. Allow them to be brutally honest about where you are and how you can mature in those areas.

# Grab On

*"Stay current and stay connected."*

# Grab On

When I was a child, if my mother said we were going to go somewhere tomorrow, it seems like tomorrow took forever to get here. I would eat breakfast and play a little bit, eat lunch and play some more, ride the bicycle, play with the skateboard or play with the dirt…only to look up and see that it is just one o'clock in the afternoon. Wow! I had the entire evening and the entire night before tomorrow would be here. You can imagine what it was like on Christmas Eve. It seemed like Christmas Eve took forever and Christmas Day took even longer to arrive. As I got older, I recognized that time was flying by. It seemed like as I aged, someone sped up the clock. Then when I had children, it seemed like one moment my daughter was being born, and the next moment I'm taking her for kindergarten orientation. Those five years flew by! Time is a tool that we have to utilize to our advantage. If you are going to GO, you must GRAB ON!

There are two areas that are key when it comes to grabbing on. One of them is staying current, and the other is staying connected. Staying current has to do with staying innovative. It has to do with being in line with what is going on now. So many people are beating a dead horse. They are trying to make things work that worked five, ten, fifteen, twenty, thirty, fifty years ago. They are caught in a time warp, and they refuse to come up to the current times. As I mentioned earlier, time is going to continue to move, whether you move with it or not. If you are going to move with it, you are going to have to grab on. Grab on to technology. You may not be the biggest fan of social media; but, I have news for you. It is not going anywhere. While you may not be on any particular social media site, 24-7, 365 days, you do have to recognize that it has become a new normal. It has literally become a new platform of communication. At one point, the radio was the only form of entertainment, and then television came. Television is being transitioned because of the demands of a quicker responding audience. Now things like live streaming are booming because of the direct to user capabilities. It is what it is.

In order for you to go, to move forward, you will have to accept the fact that times are changing. Excuse me; times have already changed. This does not change the core of who you are. It does not change the message or the messenger, but it certainly changes the method. The more efficient the method is, then the more effective the message will be. Don't allow anything to cause you to become stale. Time won't wait. The future is only a moment away. Today was tomorrow yesterday!

Now, what about staying connected? When I say get connected, I'm not talking about making sure that you have a good Wi-Fi signal. Everyone should have someone that they are connected to that can lead them toward their destiny. This someone should be leading the way in your area of interest. They should have insight that you don't have. They should be someone who is willing to show you the ropes. Whether you call this person a teacher, mentor, spiritual father, advisor or consultant; whoever this person is, you need to have one. The reason I would say stay connected where this person is concerned is because this relationship is bound to take you through loops and turns. It will take you through ups, downs, peaks, valleys, over and under. You have to be a person who is tenacious enough, who is resilient enough to stay connected. It is your responsibility to stay connected to that relationship as long as you feel that relationship is being fruitful. Remember, we are staying current, and even in those types of relationships, they may be for a season. It may not be a relationship that you should be connected to for life. You have to judge whether or not the time has lapsed. It's okay if it has. It can be very tough separating ourselves from those that we are connected to, especially if it has been an extremely long length of time. But, if the season is up, you have to shift with the season. If you don't move with the cloud *(Numbers 9:17-23)*, staying connected can be as detrimental as being connected was beneficial.

Never leave a God-given relationship because you see the latest, greatest somebody that comes up on the scene and now you want to be connected for the opportunity that it may provide. You have to make an assessment in order to make an adjustment. This principle is biblical. Jesus said that He is the vine and we are the branches. He makes an assessment that those branches that do not bear fruit will be cut off *(John 15:2)*. You and I should not have lifeless branches connected to us. What's interesting is that the same chapter he talks about cutting off lifeless branches, he talks about going and being fruitful *(John 15:16)*. Sometimes pruning is necessary for us to grow. Pruning is also necessary for us to GO. Let's GO!

## On The Go

Fruitful relationships require work! If you or the one that you are in the relationship with are not willing to put the work in, get out. No fruit can come from it. Nurture the relationships that remain. Don't allow technology to overrule the meaningful personal touch that only you can give.

# God Opportunities

*"Never confuse golden or glamour opportunities with God opportunities."*

## God Opportunities

One of the things that I believe that has brought more harm than good to us is this attitude of self-aggrandizement. In essence, it is the pursuit of promoting oneself. This can be dangerous because, in most cases, the self-promotion can cause a premature exposure to unnecessary warfare. It can cause someone that could have been great to be mediocre or to be insignificant as it relates to their pursuit, because of bad timing. They did not wait their turn. There is a reason why kindergarten comes before first grade. Kindergarten is designed to prepare the students for first grade. There is a reason why high school comes before college. High school is designed to prepare the students for college. It's really that simple. However, when our pursuits are the gold, the glamour, and the glory, our aspirations can take over. If we saw first graders sitting in a Harvard classroom, would we have to wonder why they were receiving failing grades? The obvious answer would be no. We would automatically assume that their failure had come as a result of them not being properly prepared, and we would be right!

We are in a world where people can get on a social media site and make their profile picture and name whatever they desire it to be. They can give themselves a title that they have not earned and pad their bio to say things that they have not accomplished. This is the challenge. It sounds good, but it is not sound. It will not hold water. If it is placed in a hot enough fire, it will be burned. There is purpose in the process. One of the best ways to be processed or to be properly prepared is to look for God opportunities. If you are going to GO, you are going to need GOD OPPORTUNITIES.

God opportunities are the opportunities that are designed to develop us. If you know anything about development, just like a muscle, it develops as a result of the demand that is placed on it. Resistance and heavy weight are necessary for muscles to respond with growth. I think it is important that I warn you that God opportunities are not necessarily glamour opportunities. They are not necessarily the big platforms, the big opportunities to speak or the big promotion. God opportunities may not be golden opportunities. The golden opportunities usually represent money motives. How much can I make or how can I monetize this? Sometimes the benefits of the opportunities that I am talking about do not come with any dollar amount, but what is extracted from the opportunity is priceless.

It takes a trained eye to see the God opportunities because a lot of times they are hidden. I want to help you find them. Here are a few places where God opportunities are hidden to the naked eye. If they are God opportunities, I can guarantee you that they will have one or more of the following characteristics:

1. Serving—God opportunities will give us the ability and the opportunity to serve; to be useful or beneficial to someone other than ourselves; to help someone else; to serve another person's dream in realizing their dream *(Luke 16:12)*; to give someone else the advantage. God opportunities provide that.
2. Sowing—Giving is always an indicator of a God opportunity. We have an opportunity to give of our time, our talent and of our treasure. We can even give from our tongue as we speak kind words of affirmation, bring value to others and speak life.
3. Submission—"Sub" meaning under; "mission" meaning assignment, vision and purpose; coming under the

mission, the vision, the assignment that God has for your life. Submitting to that is a place of strength. It is a place of trust. If you think about the subfloor, the carpet, the hardwood or any type of covering, no matter how attractive it is, will not be able to function the way that it was intended to function if the subfloor is ruined. A subtopic is the point that supports the overall thought or idea of what is being communicated. It is vitally important. It is not a place of weakness. It is a place of strength.

Now to the naked eye these three characteristics will not seem like opportunities at all. It sounds like you're losing and helping everyone else to win. It sounds like there is nothing there to help move your dream forward, but let's think about it. Let's look at them again.

1. Serving—"He who is <u>greatest among you</u> shall be your servant." *(Matthew 23:11)*
2. Sowing—"Give, and <u>it shall be given unto you</u>; good measure, pressed down, and shaken together, and running over, shall men give into your bosom. For with the same measure that ye mete withal it shall be measured to you again." *(Luke 6:38)*
3. Submission—"And whosoever shall exalt himself shall be abased; and he that shall humble himself <u>shall be exalted</u>." *(Matthew 23:12)*

With those things in mind, it sounds like the God opportunities are setups for acceleration. It sounds like they are the very pathways that have been paved for us to GO.

The next time you have an opportunity to serve, to sow, to submit, don't miss the God opportunity. The God opportunities will provide for you everything that you desire and more. God will give you the desires of your heart after you delight yourself in Him *(Psalm 37:4)*. He will give you what you desire, but before He does, He will give you what TO desire. Keep looking for God opportunities and you will never have to jockey for positions; you will never have to undercut anyone; you will never have to do deals under the table; you will never be looked over. Promotion does not come from man; promotion comes from God *(Psalm 75:6)*.

If you are a barber or stylist, invest time in cutting the hair of those that can't afford your services. There are plenty of kids that need what you have to offer. If you are a chef, host a low cost or free cooking class for single moms. If you are a graphic designer, find a struggling start up and provide them with promo material or a website. I think you get the point. God opportunities are everywhere. Take advantage!

## On The Go

Look for places where your gifts can be of service. Commit to serving the underserved person or group monthly for one year. Do not purposefully publicize your efforts. What you do in secret will be rewarded openly.

# Grind Obessively

*"Execution is the bridge to experience."*

## Grind Obsessively

Grind is modern vernacular that suggests working hard. You have made it to the last principle of this book. However, I could not allow you to read this book and to think that something was just going to happen because you completed it. That is not the way this works. It's true that faith without works is dead *(James 2:17)*—graveyard dead! It's true that we observe not to just say we have seen, but we must observe to do what's required for success *(Joshua 1:8)*. We are not designed just to be hearers, but we are doers also. If we don't have this type of mindset to do what we have heard, we will find ourselves in a place called self-deception *(James 1:22)*. Always remember this: a decision without a discipline is a deception. In other words, the decision is the overall desired action. It is what we have set our minds to do. The discipline represents the choices that follow that decision. It represents the steps that are necessary to see it come to pass. If the decision was a tabletop, the choices or the discipline would be the legs to that table. Without those legs, that table would come crumbling down to the ground. For us to think that tabletop will be suspended in thin air, with no legs under it, we would be deceiving ourselves. There must be a discipline attached to a decision. That discipline represents work. It will only work if you work it! If you are going to GO, you must GRIND OBSESSIVELY.

Please take real note of what I am telling you. This is something that must happen. The previous 19 chapters are all null and void if you do not adhere to this chapter. Let me start by dispelling the myth that it is not okay to work obsessively. I want to let you know that working obsessively is the only way for the believer. Hear me out. You may think I am out of balance here, but listen a little closer. What I am saying to you is you and I have been created for work. In the beginning, God did not set-up the Garden of Eden so that Adam could go there and work from nine to five. No, He placed Adam in the Garden so that he could keep it, tend to it and do whatever was necessary to fulfill the assignment. That says to me that working is a way of life. Even Jesus said that he had to work the work God had given him while he had the opportunity to do so *(John 9:4)*. We have a limited time here on earth, and it's up to us whether or not we will maximize it.

Grinding obsessively or working hard is okay. The question becomes "What am I working?" If we are going to work God's way, we need to work the assignment, the purpose, the vision, the dream that God has placed before us.

Think about it. When does God want you to take off from being purposeful? How much of a vacation would He want you to have as it relates to your assignment? As it relates to the reason why you are on the Earth? Does He want you to take a week, two weeks or a month to not do what He has told us to do? Doesn't that sound foolish? The problem becomes when we relegate work to a job; when we relegate work to our vocation rather than our divine destination. Our work should be focused on attaining everything that Christ has paid for us to have. It should be our objective to experience the best life that has been provided by the sacrificial work of Jesus Christ. I believe that Jesus paid the ultimate price in order for you and me to have the ultimate life, not the ultimate job. There is nothing wrong with a job, but it should be part of our work. If it is our home life, we have to work that. Grinding obsessively means that we do 100% of the work that is required for the area that we are involved in at the time. If it is parenting, we have to work that.

If it is ministry, we have to work that. If it is on our job, we have to work that. If it is our recreational or leisure time, we have to work that. We always have something that we can do that is necessary for us to be all that God has called us to be.

I am not attempting to make you a person who is out of balance. Balance is the key to life. I am simply telling you that even if you could divide your day into equal portions for every part of your life, if you did not provide equal work, you still would not have the fruit that you desire in the areas that you desire them. Work represents execution and execution is the key. It is my opinion that this has been one of the major keys that have held us back from maximizing who we have been designed to be…as kings, as priests, as children of God, as heirs, as those who have been given authority, power and dominion, we have lost it in our failure to execute.

We have the EXPLANATION. If we don't know, it is because we don't want to know. With things like the Internet, it is really not that difficult to ask our buddy, Google, to give us what we need. He would probably not only give you the answer but before you complete the request, he would complete the sentence for you. I'm in agreement with my mentor, Apostle Amos L. Howard, Sr., who says, "You have to want to be dumb, to be dumb in these times that we live in." We have plenty of explanations.

We also have EXAMPLES. We have people who have lived the principles, who have walked them out, who have seen them happen in their lives. We have people like me, who are telling you that these things work not because of what they have heard, but because of what they have experienced.

God knows we have plenty of EXCITEMENT. It is nothing for us to find something that can "gas us up" or that can get us to a place where we feel like we can conquer the world. With explanation, examples and excitement that creates expectations, it's still not enough to carry us over to experience. Execution is the bridge to experience.

If there is no execution, if we are not willing to do what others have done, if we are not willing to do what is necessary to fulfill our dreams, we will find ourselves in an invisible prison of limitations. We are going to find ourselves seeing the great vast abundance, but never attaining it. We have to put in the work. We have to strategically and intentionally make every effort to do what we have learned to do. It is not what we do one time, two times, three times, four or five times. It has to become a way of living. When it does, no one will be able to stop us, except us. Let's GO!

## On The Go

List the top 5 roles and responsibilities that you hold. Under each area identify 5 things that you can "DO" to improve how you function in that role. To be better at your role as a parent you might consider investing a set amount of hours with your children each week. Then, look at each area individually and identify ways to prevent them from overlapping. How can you be totally present in the current role so that you give 100% to the task at hand? Maybe the current role is being a spouse and doing better means no use of cell phones, laptops or tablets in the bedroom. Whatever the task is, you must put in the work to receive the reward.

## CONCLUSION

To GO is to refrain from excuse making and live life in action mode. To GO is to recognize that each waking moment of everyday is an opportunity to take a step up from where you currently are. To GO is to realize that success or failure is dependent on if you move. GO!!!

## MINING THE GOLD

- Don't be a moment chaser. Be a moment maker!

- The ability to see things properly and clearly are keys to you moving forward.

- Maximized moments make momentum and maintained momentum makes a movement.

- Never confuse the enemy with the inner-me.

- Gifts are not decided; they are discovered.

- Exposure expands your expectations

- Goals don't have to be massive; but they do have to be measurable.

- Any area that you're not willing to execute is the same area that you're not willing to experience.

- Only say what you want to see in your life.

- Don't allow anyone to have automatic placement in your circle of influence.

- A decision without a discipline is a deception.

## ABOUT THE AUTHOR

Tymetric Dillon is a native of Milwaukee, Wisconsin. He left the comforts of his home city where he had family, friends and business success, to pursue purpose and fulfillment. While on his journey he built many meaningful relationships and learned important life lessons. His connection to people and commitment to principles has given him profound insights that he is able to translate into practical steps toward success.

He has proven himself to be a man of vision, integrity and character that lives the principles that he teaches. His mission is to liberate and build people by communicating a relevant message of faith and freedom that helps people to live their best life.

He has a wife and three children.

*TYMETRIC DILLON*

*G.O.*

*TYMETRIC DILLON*

www.ingramcontent.com/pod-product-compliance
Lightning Source LLC
Chambersburg PA
CBHW071531080526
44588CB00011B/1638